T0209741

The One True And Living God

DR. JOHN THOMAS WYLIE

authorHOUSE®

AuthorHouse™
1663 Liberty Drive
Bloomington, IN 47403
www.authorhouse.com
Phone: 1 (800) 839-8640

Published by AuthorHouse 09/04/2019

ISBN: 978-1-7283-2624-5 (sc)
ISBN: 978-1-7283-2623-8 (e)

Print information available on the last page.

This book is printed on acid-free paper.

The Holy Bible (1964) Authorized King James Version. Chicago, Ill.: J. G. Ferguson

The Holy Bible (1953) The Revised Standard Version. Nashville, TN.: Thomas Nelson
And Sons (Used By Permission)

The Holy Bible (1901) The American Standard
Version. Nashville, Tn.: Thomas Nelson
(Used By Permission)

The Holy Bible (1959) The Berkeley Version. Grand Rapids, MI.: Zondervan
(Used By Permission)

The Holy Bible (2017) The New Testament Version. Grand Rapids, MI.: Zondervan
(Used By Permission)

The New Testament In Modern English (1958) J. B.
Philips, New York, NY: Macmillian
(Used By Permission)

The New Testament In The Language Of The People (1937, 1949) Chicago, Ill.:
Charles B. Williams, Bruce Humphries, Inc. Moody Bible Institute
(Used By Permission)

Contents

CHAPTER THREE

CHAPTER FOUR

CHAPTER FIVE

CHAPTER NINE

Introduction

There Is One True And Living God

As LIMITED CREATURES WE can't seek after unlimited knowledge. As corrupt creatures our brains don't work flawlessly. We are evacuated in dialect, topography, and time from the world in which the occasions of Biblical history occurred. The wonder isn't that we are astounded at so much, but that so much is obvious to us. Paul stated, "Now we see through a glass, obscurely" (I Cor. 13:12), and, "We know to some extent" (I Cor. 13:9). These contemplations are material to concentrate the Scriptures.

The Christian who approaches Scripture with a determined reliance on the Holy Spirit, and a will to know God's will, will discover his life going up against another measurement. Never ready to flaunt flawlessness, he will in any case develop to spiritual maturity as he benefits from the wealth of Scripture and believe in faith.

This publication, "There Is One True And Living God," does not endeavor to demonstrate there is a God but rather has inside it's pages the things that assist men to know "There Is One True and Living God."

The Bible being God's disclosure or God's Revelation to man, God speaks from the very first page. The Bible does not address the presence of God by unique thinking, however starts with the simple demonstration of Creation.

The Bible does not endeavor to demonstrate that there is a God. Men wherever definitely know there is a God. One Who is head over all things. But then, people wonder about Who this God is and might want to know many other things about Him.

Reverend Dr. John Thomas Wylie

Chapter
ONE

Man Knows There Is A God Because Of What He Sees Around Him

How did this world appear? It couldn't appear independent from anyone else. Who made it? There is no mystery about it. God's Word tells who made the world. "In the beginning "God" made from nothing the heavens and the earth" (Gen. 1:1). The sky above man and the earth around him demonstrate that Someone made them. This did not simply occur. At the point when man makes something, he utilizes things to make different things.

But, God did not use anything to make the world. "Let them praise the name of the Lord! For He spoke and they appeared" (Psalm 148:5). These things around man don't reveal to him Who made the world. In any case, they do disclose to him that Whoever made it was more than exceptionally, extraordinary, great.

Man Knows There Is A God Because All Things Work As They Were Planned

Think about the earth, sun, moon and stars. They don't keep running into one another. They go quite a long time in the manner in which they were intended to go! A large number of stars were placed in their places. Evenings and days travel every which way dependably as they were arranged. Summers and winters go back and forth dependably as they were arranged.

The One who arranged this had incredible wisdom. In Psalm 19:1 we read, "The sky are recounting the enormity of God and the incredible open spaces above demonstrate crafted by His hands." God's Word additionally says in Romans 1:20, "Men can't say they don't know in regards to God. From the earliest beginning point of the world, men could perceive what God is like through the things He has made. This demonstrates His power that keeps going forever. It demonstrates that He is God.

Man Knows There Is A God Because Of The Way People Are Made

THE ONE WHO BROUGHT man into being must be more prominent than man. Man can know believe and act. Man has something inside him that discloses to him when he has fouled up. He isn't just flesh, blood, and bones, man can know ideal from off-base. This makes him know there is an All-Powerful God who made man and rules over him.

"When I turn upward and consider Your sky, created by Your fingers, the moon and the stars, which You have set in their place, what is man, that You consider him, the child of man that You care for him? You made him somewhat less than the heavenly angels and gave him a crown of greatness and honor. You made him rule over the works created by Your hands.

You put everything under his feet. All sheep and steers, all the wild creatures, the feathered creatures of the air, and fish of the ocean, and all that go through the ocean. O Lord, our Lord, how extraordinary is Your name in all the earth" (Psalm 8:3-9).

Man Knows There Is A God Because Of What The Past Tells Him

MAN KNOWS THE BOOK of scriptures is the Word of God. Early evangelists said certain things would occur later on, and they happened. Christ came to earth by a ground-breaking work to accomplish something extraordinary for men. The disciples of Christ have taken the Good News around the globe as the years progressed. Men's lives have been changed as they have put their trust in Christ.

Corrupt men, sinful men have never possessed the capacity (power) to pulverize what God has made. These things must be done through God's power and work. "The rulers of the earth remain in a line prepared to battle, and every one of the pioneers are against the Lord and against His Chosen One (Jesus Christ). They say, "Given us a chance to break their chains and discard them from us." He who sits in paradise giggles. "The Lord makes fun of them" (Psalm 2:2-4).

Man Knows There Is A God Because All Men Know They Need A God

EACH INDIVIDUAL KNOWS THERE is something incorrect in his/her life. He may not call it sin, but rather he has a liable inclination. Each individual knows there must be One Who is impeccable. He knows there must be Someone Who is head over all. Man needs a leader. The Word of God does not endeavor to demonstrate there is a God.

It just tells about God since men over all the world definitely realize that He is. The Word of God lets us know there is just a single true God. "The Lord our God is one Lord" (Deuteronomy 6:4; Mark 12:29b. Isaiah 44:6b says "...There is no God other than Me." God is the Head over all things. He is the one and only True and Living God.

Chapter

TWO

The Names Of God

IN NUMEROUS PARTS OF the world a name given to a man has an importance. In Bible occasions names had unique significance. They were given to specific individuals for specific reasons. The names of God demonstrate what He is like. They indicate how He acts and functions among the general population He made.

Men should recognize what they intended to the general population long ago and what they can mean today. Knowing the names of God can enable man to know God better. His name is more prominent than some other name. The Old Testament was composed in the Hebrew dialect and the three imperative names for God are in that dialect. The names given beneath are the names in English.

The Three Most Important Names Of God In The Old Testament

GOD - THIS NAME implies The Power That Rules. In the plain first verse of the Bible this word is utilized. "In the beginning God made from nothing the heavens and the earth" (Genesis 1:1). This power made the world and rules over it.

LORD - This name is composed in extensive letters. It isn't the equivalent as Lord. It implies Life or The One Who Always Has Been, Is Now, And Always Will Be. It likewise intends To Be and The One Who Needs Nothing and The Coming One. In Exodus 3:14 God said to Moses, "I AM WHO I AM."

Lord - This is the name which demonstrates that God is Ruler over men and that men put themselves under God's rule and trust Him (Genesis 15:2). It implies Owner or Husband. John 13:13 understands, "You call Me Teacher and Lord. You are correct on the grounds that that is the thing that I am." And in II Corinthians 11:2,3 a similar word implies Husband. Ruler can be utilized for a man, but then a little "L" is used.

Other Important Names
Of God In The Bible

ALL-POWERFUL GOD - IMPLIES The Strong One and The God Who Is Enough and The One Who Gives Strength and The Strong One Who Sees and The God Who Has Power Over All (Genesis 16:13;17:1-20).

Most High God - implies The Highest or The One Who claims Heaven and Earth. Isaiah 66:1a says, "The Lord says, "Paradise is My throne, and the earth is where I rest My feet" (Deuteronomy 32:8; Psalm 83:18; Acts 7:48-50).

God Who Lasts Forever - implies that God will never die. It likewise implies that He is the God Who is over things that keep going forever. Psalm 90:2 says, "Before the mountains were conceived, before You brought forth the earth and world, for all eternity, You are God." "You made the earth at the outset.; You made the heavens with Your hands. They will be devastated however You will in every case live" (Psalm 102:25,26a).

LORD God - is first utilized in Genesis 2:4. This name is utilized two different ways: (1) God as producer (maker) of man (Genesis 2:7); God as a pioneer of Israel (Genesis 24:7; Exodus 3:15; Deuteronomy 12:1). It is utilized as Owner and Leader and The One Who Saves. And after that it is additionally utilized when God talked or promised things to His Chosen people. Some of the time it is composed Lord God. This implies Owner.

LORD of All - is a name of God showing His power and shining greatness in war, and also in caring for others (Samuel 17:45; Psalm 46:7, 11; Isaiah 47:4).

Names Of God Used In The Old Testament Which Tell About Him And How He Works

THE LORD WHO WILL Give What Is Needed - This Name implies The Lord Will Take Care of Our Needs. This name was utilized when Abraham was going to give his son as a blessing on the sacrificial stone (altar) to God (Genesis 22:13,14).

The LORD Who Heals - He is the One Who heals men's bodies from sickness and disease (Exodus 15:26).

The LORD Who wins For Us – It is God Who fights against Satan for man (Exodus 17:8-15).

The LORD Our Peace – It is God Who gives Peace (Judges 6:24).

The LORD My Shepherd – God is the One Who leads men through hard places (See Psalm 23).

The Lord - God's Life In Us – This speaks of the day when Christ will be King of the earth, but Christ's life is now in those who have put their trust in Him (Jeremiah 23:6 I Corinthians 1:30).

The LORD Is Here Now – This name also looks forward to the day Christ will be king of the earth (Ezekiel 48:35; Revelation 11:15; 17:14; 20:4; 21:3).

The Lord Is The One Who Sets Us Apart and Makes Us Holy (Exodus 31:13; Leviticus 20:26).

The Lord Is The One Who Makes Us Right With Himself (Jeremiah 23:6).

God Is The One Who Will Pay Back or The Lord Will Punish And Pay Back (Jeremiah 51:56; Ezekiel 7:9; Romans 12:19).

The names that bring all the others together and make them complete are "Alpha" and "Omega." These are the first and last Greek letters and mean the First and Last, the Beginning and End of all things. The names of God are used in many different parts of God's Word (Revelation 1:8) One part that uses many of these different names is Psalm 23. (Read Psalm 23).

God Is Everywhere

THERE IS NO PLACE that God isn't. Man must not consider God having a body like his. Regardless of whether man peruses of God having ears, eyes, feet, or a right side, it must be comprehended this discusses Him having the power to see, hear, and feel wherever in the meantime.

Man can't see how enormous God is. The heaven are not sufficiently huge for Him. II Chronicles 6:18b says, "...See, paradise and the most astounding paradise can't hold You. How substantially less would this be able to house hold You which I have fabricated." Heaven, heck, all aspects of the ocean, all haziness and all light are brimming with God. What's more, God isn't a long way from every single one of the individuals who are His children.

Acts 17:27 says, "They were to search for God. At that point they may feel after Him and discover Him since He isn't a long way from every last one of us." There is no place man can abandon God being there. In Jeremiah 23:24 it says, "Can a man shroud himself in mystery puts with the goal that I can't see him?" says the Lord.

"Do I not fill paradise and earth?" says the Lord." God is wherever in light of the fact that He is Spirit. However, there is an exceptional place called paradise where God is. Matthew 5:34,35 tells where God is. "I let you know, don't utilize solid words when you make a guarantee. Try not to guarantee by paradise. It is where God is.

Try not to guarantee by paradise. It is where God is. Try not to guarantee by earth. It is where God rests his feet.

Try not to guarantee by Jerusalem. It is the city of the incomparable King." While Stephen was being slaughtered, he said in Acts 7:56, "Behold! I see paradise open and the Son of Man remaining at the correct side of God!" (Psalm 139:7-10).

Chapter

THREE

Certain Things About God That He Does Not Share With Man

It is difficult to comprehend the contrast between God's identity and what God is like. Here we plan to demonstrate the distinction:

God Always Was And Always Will Be.

Since everything has a beginning and an end, it is difficult to see how God had no beginning. He always was. God is without beginning or end. He is the "I AM." He is always the same. In Revelation 1:8 it says, "The Lord God says, "I am the First and the Last, the beginning and the end of all things." I am the All-powerful One Who was and Who is and Who is to come.'

What's more, in Psalm 90:2 it says, "Before the mountains were conceived, before You brought forth the earth and the world, forever and ever, You are God" (Isaiah 41:4b).

God Never Changes.

Whenever something transforms (changes), it is to improve things or for the more awful. Be that as it may, God can't improve in light of the fact that He is as of now perfect. He can't change for the more terrible in light of the fact that He is God. Malachi 3:6 says, "For I, the Lord, don't change." James 1:17 says, "Whatever is great and perfect comes to us from God. He is the One Who made all light. He doesn't change. No shadow is made by His turning (Psalm 33:11).

God Knows All Things.

God knows Himself and He know every other thing. He knows everything that will happen to man. He knows whether man will put his trust in His Son, or get some distance from (turn away from) Him (Genesis 15:13-15; Exodus 3:7-9; Ecclesiastes 12:14; Luke 12:2; I Corinthians 4:5; I Peter 1:10-12).

God comprehends what a man is thinking about. I Chronicles 28:9 says, "...For the Lord investigates all hearts, and sees each arrangement and thought..." No idea can be kept from God. Job 42:2 says, "I realize that You can do all things. Nothing can put a stop to Your designs." And in Psalm 139:2 it says, "You know when I take a seat and when I get up. You comprehend my considerations from far away."

There isn't a word that originates from the mouth of man without the Lord knowing it. Psalm 139:4 says, "Even before I speak a word, O Lord, You know everything."

We may not think about specific things that we should let him know, yet He knows all things. I John 3:20 says, "Our heart may state that we have fouled up. Be that as it may, recollect, God is more prominent than our heart. He knows everything." "For the methods for a man are seen by the eyes of the Lord, and He observes every one of his ways" (Proverbs 5:21).

The plan God has for man to be saved from the punishment of sin is more prominent than anything man can consider. In Romans 11:33 it says, "God's riches are so extraordinary" The things He knows and His wisdom are so profound. Nobody can comprehend His considerations. Nobody can comprehend His ways" (Isaiah 55:7; 64:4; I Corinthians 2:9).

God knows every person.

He has made and knows every little thing about them. In Matthew 10:29,30 it says, "Are not two little winged creatures sold for a little bit of cash? But not one of the flying creatures tumbles to the earth without your Father knowing it. God knows what number of hairs you have on your head" (Psalm 33:13-15; Jeremiah 1:5).

God witnesses everything that is in each place.

In Hebrews 4:13 it says, "Nobody can escape God. His eyes see all that we do. We should give a response to God for what we have done" (Proverbs 15:3 says, "The eyes of the Lord are in each place, viewing the terrible and the great" (Proverbs 5:21).

God knows every one of the distresses of men.

"The Lord stated, "I have seen the enduring of My people in Egypt. I have heard their cry on account of the men who make them work. I know how they suffer" (Exodus 3:7).

God knows everything that have occurred before and everything that will occur later on (Isaiah 46:9,10; Acts 2:23; Romans 8:27-29).

God Knows All Things

Acts 1:24 - "At that point the followers prayed, saying, "Lord, you know the hearts everything being equal. Demonstrate to us which of these two men You have picked" (I Samuel 16:7).

Acts 15:8 - "God knows the hearts all things considered.

He indicated them they were to have His loving support by giving them the Holy Spirit the equivalent as He provided for us." Pharaoh would not release the Israelites (Exodus 3:19).

I Corinthians 3:20 - "They likewise say, The Lord knows how the wise men think. His reasoning merits nothing (Psalm 94:11).

II Timothy 2:19 - "Yet reality of God can't be changed. It says, The Lord realizes the individuals who are His.' And Everyone who says he is a Christian must turn from sin!"

Romans 8:29 - "God knew from the earliest starting point who might put their trust in Him. So He picked them and made them to be His Son. Christ was first, and each one of the individuals who have a place with God are His brothers."

God Is All-Powerful

HE CAN DO ALL that He needs to do. His power has no closure. Nothing can change or stop God's power. At the point when God says He will accomplish something, He will do it (Numbers 23:19).

Men can do a few things, yet they can't do all things. In Matthew 19:16 it says, "Jesus took a look at them and stated, "This is impossible by men. Yet, with God all things are possible" (Job 42:2).

God can do things that are difficult to accept. Luke 1:36,37 says, "See, your cousin Elizabeth, as old as she seems to be, will bring forth a youngster. She was not ready to have children previously, but rather now she is in her 6th month. For God can do all things" (Genesis 18:14).

God does give life, as well as breath life into a man back after death (Acts 26:8 says, "For what reason do you think it is difficult to trust that God raises individuals from the dead?" John 11:43,44 says, "When He had said this, He called with an uproarious voice, 'Lazarus, come out!' The man who had been dead came out. His situation is practically hopeless in grave garments. A white material was tied around his face. Jesus said to the general population, "Remove the grave garments and release him!" (I Kings 17:22; II Kings 4:32-34; John 11:1-44).

God Is Everywhere

There is no place where God isn't. Man must not consider God having a body like his. Regardless of whether man peruses of God having ears, feet, or a correct side, it must be comprehended this discusses Him having the capacity to see, hear, and feel wherever in the meantime.

Man can't see how enormous God is. The heaven are not sufficiently enormous for Him. II Chronicles 6:18b says, "...See, paradise and the most noteworthy paradise can't hold You. How substantially less would this be able to house hold You which I have assembled." Heaven, hell, all aspects of the ocean, all darkness and all light are loaded with God.

Furthermore, God isn't a long way from every last one of the individuals who are His children. Acts 17:27 says, "They were to search for God. At that point they may feel after Him and discover Him since He isn't a long way from every single one of us." "There is no place man can abandon God being there.

In Jeremiah 23:24 it says, "Can a man conceal himself in secret puts with the goal that I can't see him?" says the Lord. "Do I not fill paradise and earth?" says the Lord." God is wherever on the grounds that He is Spirit. Be that as it may, there is a unique place called paradise where God is. Matthew 5:34,35 tells where God is.

"I let you know, don't utilize strong words when you make a promise. Try not to promise by paradise. It is where God is. Try not to promise by earth. It is the place He rest His feet. Try not to promise by Jerusalem. It is the city of the incomparable King." While Stephen was being slaughtered, he said in Acts 7:56, "See! I see paradise open and the Son of Man standing at the right side of God!" (Psalm 139:7-10).

Chapter
FOUR

Certain Things About God That He Shares With Man

In Chapter Three we were instructed how God did not impart certain things to man. In this section it very well may be perceived how God has certain things that He pronounces to impart to man. man does not have these things himself. After he becomes a Christian and wants to live for Him, God shares these things.

God Is Holy

"Holy - means to be free from all sin, or to be unadulterated. In I Peter 1:13 it says, "Be blessed in all aspects of your life. Be like the Holy One Who chose you." God is Holy and willing to share this with man.

When man resembles God in this way, it implies he is separate for God-like living and set apart to work for God. In John 17:11b it says, "Holy Father, keep those You have given to Me in the in the power of Your name." God speaks of Himself as being holy in I Peter 1:16 when He says, "You should be holy, for I am Holy" (Joshua 24:19; Psalm 99:5,9).

Luke 1:49, "He who is powerful has done great things for me. His name is holy" (Isaiah 57:15).

Revelation 4:8 - "Every last one of the four living creatures had six wings. They had eyes all over them, all around. Day and night they say constantly, "Holy, holy, holy is the Lord, the All-powerful One. He is the One Who was and Who is and Who is to come" (Isaiah 6:3)

Revelation 6:10 - "Each one of the individuals who had been killed shouted out with a boisterous voice saying, "To what extent will it be yet before You will punish those on the earth for murdering us? Lord, You are holy and true." (Deuteronomy 32:43; Psalm 79:10).

Revelation 18:4 - "Who will not honor You, O Lord, with love and fear? Who will tell the greatness of Your name? For You are the only One Who is Holy. All countries will come and worship before You. Everybody sees that You do the right things" (Psalm 86:9; Jeremiah 10:7).

God Is Always Right And Whatever He Does Is Good

GOD MADE A WAY for man to be ideal with Himself. God will pardon and get the delinquent (sinner) who gets through Jesus' passing on the cross. In I Corinthians 1:30 it says, "God Himself made the way so you to can have new life through Jesus Christ. God gave us Christ to be our knowledge (wisdom). Jesus Christ made us right with God, and separate us for God and made us blessed. Christ bought us with His blood and made us free from our transgressions (sins)" (Psalm 19:9; Jeremiah 23:5).

God Is Always Faithful And True

GOD CAN SIMPLY BE trusted. In I Corinthians 10:13 it advises how God is faithful to His children. "You have never been enticed to sin in any unexpected route in comparison to other individuals. God is faithful. He won't enable you to be tempted more than you can take. Be that as it may, when you are tempted, He will make a path for you to keep from falling into wrongdoing (sin)."

God is steadfast, faithful in what He promised. In I Thessalonians 5:24 it says, "The One Who called you is faithful and will do what He promised." And in Hebrews 10:23 it says, "Given us a chance to clutch the expectation we say we have and not be changed. We can confide in God that He will do what He promised." And He is faithful to Himself. In II Timothy 2:13 it says, "If we have no faith, He will in any case be faithful for He can't conflict with what He is" (Deuteronomy 7:9; Isaiah 49:7).

God Is A God Of Loving-Pity And Loving-Kindness

THIS IS LIKEWISE FOUND in the Christian who wants to please God. In Romans 2:4 it says, "Do you disregard His cherishing benevolence to you? Do you overlook to what extent He is sitting tight for you? You realize that God is caring. He is attempting to persuade you to be sad for your transgressions (sins) and abandon them." In Romans 11:22 it says, "We perceive how kind

God is. It indicates how hard He is moreover. He is challenging for the individuals who fall away. Be that as it may, He is benevolent to you in the event that you continue confiding in Him. If you don't. He will cut you off" (Psalm 89:24).

God Is Love

THE VAST MAJORITY CONSIDER God a God of love. Genuine love is from God and the Christian has love for others since God gives him love. The Christian method for worship is the way of worship that says God is love. The false gods forces of wood, stone, and different things that numerous individuals worship in numerous parts of the world are believed to be brimming with hate.

These individuals think something must be given to these false gods constantly so the false gods won't punish them. The individuals who put their trust in God's Son, Jesus Christ, are loved by God (Deuteronomy 7:7,8; Jeremiah 31:3; II Corinthians 5:14a; 13:11b).

I John 4:8-16 - "The individuals who don't love don't know God since God is love. God has demonstrated His love to us by sending His Only

Son into the world. God did this so we may have life through Christ. This is love! It isn't that we loved God but that He loved us.

For God sent His Son to pay for our wrongdoings (our sins) with His blood. Dear companions, if God loved us that much, at that point we should love one another. No individual has ever seen God at any time. In the event that we love one another, God lives in us. His love is made perfect in us. He has given us His Spirit.

This is the manner by which we realize we live by His assistance and He lives in us. We have seen and can state that the Father sent His Son to spare the world from the discipline of transgression. The individual who recounts Him before men and says that Jesus is the Son of God, God is living in that one and that one is living by the assistance of God. We have come to know and trust the affection God has for us. God is love. On the off chance that you live infatuated, you live by the assistance of God and God lives in you."

John 14:21 - "The person who adores Me is the person who has My instructing and obeys it. My Father will love whoever cherishes Me.

I will love them and will show Myself to him" (Deuteronomy 10:12; Proverbs 8:17).

John 16:27 - "...because the Father cherishes you. He cherishes you since you adore Me and trust that I originated from the Father.

John 17:23, 26 - "I am in them and You are in Me so they be one and be made impeccable. At that point the world may realize that You sent Me and that You cherish them as You adore Me." "I have made your name known to them and will make it known. So then the affection You have for Me might be in them and I might be in them."

God loves the universe of men, despite the fact that they are corrupt. John 3:16 says, "For God so loveed the world that He gave His Only Son. Whoever put his trust in God's Son won't be lost, yet will have life that keeps going forever." Romans 5:8 says, "However God demonstrated His love to us. While we were still heathens (sinners), Christ died for us." God dealt with the transgression (sin) issue by giving His Son (Isaiah 53:5,6).

Romans 1:7 - "So I keep in touch with every one of you in the city of Rome. God loves you and has chosen you to be separate for Himself. May God our Father and the Lord Jesus Christ give you His loving support and harmony" (Psalm 91:14).

Romans 5:8 - "However God demonstrated His love to us. While we were still miscreants (sinners), Christ died for us" (Isaiah 53:6).

Galatians 2:20 - "I have been set up on the cross to die with Christ. I never again live. Christ lives in me. The existence I presently live in this body, I live by putting my trust in the Son of God. He was simply the One Who loveed me and gave Himself for Me."

Ephesians 2:4 - "However God had so much loving thoughtfulness. He loved us with such an extraordinary love" (Nehemiah 9:17b).

Hebrews 12:6 - "The Lord punishes everybody He loves. He sends each child He gets" (Psalm 119:75; Proverbs 3:11,12).

I John 3:1 - "See what incredible love the Father has for us that He would call us His children. Also, that is the thing that we are. Hence the general population of the world don't know our identity since they didn't have any acquaintance with Him.

These things God imparts to men who have been saved from the punishment of sin, and want to carry on with a God-like life.

Chapter FIVE

What God Is Like

Since God is The sort of person He is, words are difficult to tell about Him. The Word of God enables man to think about Him and what He is like. It isn't conceivable to disclose Who God is without telling what He is like and what He does.

God Is Spirit

God does not have a body. On account of Who He is and how He functions. He needn't bother with a body like a person. In John 4:24 it says, "God is Spirit. The individuals who worship Him must worship Him in Spirit and in truth" (Deuteronomy 4:15; Psalm 139:7).

God Is Light

This tells what He is like and how He functions. The main thing He did after He made the world was to make light." And God stated, 'Let there be light,' and there was light" (Genesis 1:3). In I John 1:5 it says, "This is the thing that we heard Him let us know. We are passing it on to

you. God is light. There is no darkness in Him"
(Isaiah 60:19).

God Is Love

GOD ISN'T ONLY BRIMMING with love, He is love.
He is glad to impart His love to man. In I John
4:16 it says, "We have come to know and trust
the love God has for us. God is love. If you live
in love, you live by the assistance of God and
God lives in you." (God cherishes man yet He
hates sin. Proverbs 6:16-19) (Isaiah 43:4; Jeremiah
31:3).

God Is A Fire Who
Destroys What Is Sinful

GOD IS RIGHT IN all that He does. He is holy
and perfect. Whenever silver and gold are made
unadulterated so no other metal is blended with
them, a hot fire is utilized to consume with
extreme heat everything that isn't good. Fire
cleans. In Hebrews 12:29 it says, "For our God
is a fire that destroys everything" (Deuteronomy
4:24; 9:3,19).

God Is A Person

THE THREE THINGS THAT make a person are: (1) The power of knowing, (2) The power of feeling, and (3) The power of choosing. God has these three things and He is a person. He doesn't have a body since He is Spirit. Spirits don't have bodies. We realize He is a person in light of the fact that:

We know He Is A Person Because God Has The Power Of Knowing

GOD KNOWS HIMSELF. WHEN He called Moses from the burning bush, He stated, "I AM WHO I AM." It could be said no more grounded. God was certain of Himself. God knows all things. In Acts 15:18 it says, "God has made every one of His works known from the earliest beginning point of time." And Hebrews 4:13 says, 'Nobody can avoid God. His eyes see all that we do." (II Chronicles 16:9; Psalm 33:13-15).

We Know He Is A Person Because God Has The Power Of Feeling

THE VERSE THAT SHOWS this best is John 3:16, "For God so loved the world..." And James 5:11b says, "The Lord is full of loving-kindness and pity." (Psalm 103:8).

We Know He Is A Person Because God Has The Power Of Choosing

PSALM 115:3 SAYS, "BUT our God is in the heavens. He does whatever He wants to do." (Psalm 103:19).

God Does Not Change

NOTHING CAN CHANGE HIM or His activities. He has no beginning and He will dependably be. God dependably has been the equivalent and dependably will be the equivalent. In Malachi 3:6a it says, "For I, the Lord, don't change." It likewise says in James 1:17a, "Whatever is good and perfect comes to us from God. He is the One Who made all light. He doesn't change." Hebrews 6:17-18 says, "Thus God made a promise. He needed to shoe Abraham that He could never change His mind. So He made the promise in His own name. God gave these two things that can't be changed and God can't lie. We who have turned to Him can have extraordinary solace realizing that He will do what He has promised." (I Samuel 15:29).

God Is All Wisdom

GOD ISN'T ONLY WISE, but He knows all things. He utilizes what He knows in a way that is right and good. In Romans 11:33 it says, "God's riches are so extraordinary! The things He knows and His intelligence are so profound! Nobody can comprehend His thoughts. Nobody can comprehend His ways." (Psalm 104:24; Daniel 2:20).

God Is All-Powerful

THERE IS NOTHING GOD cannot do. Matthew 19:26 says, "But with God all things can be done. (Jeremiah 32:17).

God Is Holy And Perfect

ALL THAT HE DOES is right and good. In I Peter 1:15,16 it says, "Be holy in all aspects of your life. Be holy like the Holy One Who chose you. The Holy Writings say, 'You should be holy, for I am holy.'...Also in John 17:11 it says, "I am no longer in the world. I am coming to you. Be that as it may, these things are still in the world. Holy Father, keep those You have given to Me in the power of Your Name. At that point they will be one, even as We are One.' (Deuteronomy 32:4; Psalm 18:30a).

God Is Truth

IN JOHN 3:33 IT says, "Whoever get His words demonstrates that God is true." Part of Romans 3:4 says, "God is in every case genuine regardless of whether each man lies." I John 5:6,7 says "Jesus Christ came by water and blood. He didn't come by water only, however by water and blood.

The Holy Spirit talks about this and He is truth. There are three who talk about this in paradise: the Father and the Word and the Holy Spirit., These three are one." (Isaiah 65:16).

God Is The One Who Brings Everything Into Being, Keeps It, And Brings It To Its End

Everything is under God's extraordinary, great power, and He is the One Who is head over all things. In Isaiah 45:5-7 it says, "I am the Lord, and there is no other. There is no God other than me. I will give you strength, despite the fact that you have not known me. At that point men may know from dawn to nightfall that there is no God other than Me. I am the Lord, and there is no other. I make the light, and I make darkness. I bring great and I make trouble. I am the Lord Who does every one of these things." Colossians 1:17b says, "Everything is held together by Him."

Chapter
SIX

The Three In One
God (The Trinity)

THE THREE-IN-ONE GOD OR "Trinity" implies
that there is one God in three persons as: God The
Father, God The Son, and God The Holy Spirit.
The Trinity! This is difficult to comprehend,
but then the Word of God recounts one God
in three persons. This may help. A substantial
gathering of individuals getting together is called
one gathering.

A few grapes become together and are called
one cluster. The couple are one. Matthew 19:5
says, "Hence a man will leave his father and his
mother and will live with his wife. The two will
become one."

Matthew 3:16,17 demonstrates the three
different persons. "At the point when Jesus left the
water, the heavens opened. He saw the Spirit of
God descending and laying on Jesus like a dove.
A voice was gotten notification from paradise. It
stated, "This is My much-adored (Beloved Son)
Son. I am exceptionally content with Him." "The
Father speaks from paradise, the Son is purified
through water in the Jordan River, and Jesus

discloses to His followers to sanctify through water new Christians for the sake of the Father, and the Son, and the Holy Spirit.

Paul closes his letter to the Christians in the city of Corinth by saying in II Corinthians 13:14, "May you have cherishing support from our Lord Jesus Christ. May you have the love for God. May you be combined by the Holy Spirit.

In John 14:16a Jesus says, "I will ask My Father and He will give you another helper." Jesus is requesting that the Father give the Holy Spirit. In Romans 1:7 it talks about the Father Who is God. In Hebrews 1:5 the Son Who is God; and In Acts 5:3,4 the Holy Spirit Who is God. Not one of the three Persons is more prominent or not exactly the others, and there can never be a division among them.

It might comprehend by considering it along these lines:

The Father is God, the part of the Three-in-one God Who isn't seen (John 1:18) The Son is God, the part of the Three-in-one God Who left paradise to live in human substance among evil men (John 1:14-18). The Holy Spirit is God, the part of the Three-in-one God Who works in and through men (I Corinthians 2:9,10).

Chapter
SEVEN

The Works Of God

WORKS BY GOD ARE what He has done previously, what He is doing now, and what He will do later on. In Romans 1:20 it says, "Men can't say they don't know in regards to God. From the earliest beginning point of the world, men could perceive what God is like through the things He has made. This demonstrates His power that keeps going forever. It demonstrates that He is God."

They see his works. Be that as it may, to realize His works isn't the equivalent as knowing His ways. His works might be known by the individuals who think about Him. In any case, His ways are referred to by the individuals who know Him as a man. "He made know His ways to Moses, and His demonstrations (works) to the offspring of Israel." Work by God demonstrate His arrangement for all occasions. In I Timothy 1:17 it says, "We give respect and on account of the King Who lives until the end of time. He is the One Who never dies and Who is never seen. He is the One Who Knows all things. He is the only God. Leave it alone so."

In Ephesians 1:11 it says, "We were already chosen to be God's own children by Christ.

This was done simply like the arrangement He had." It can be perceived how everything fills in as He arranged it. God works similarly as He designs. This is found in Ephesians 3:11. "This was the arrangement God had forever. He did this through Christ Jesus our Lord."

God Made (Brought Into Being) Everything

THE WORD CREATION IS utilized in many variants. It implies created by the Three-in-one God by which in the first place and for His very own sparkling significance. He made (created), without the utilization of anything that was previously, the entire world that can be seen and that which can't be seen (Genesis 1:1,2; John 1:1,3).

It Can Be Seen That Every Work Of God Is Done By The Three-In-One God

GOD THE FATHER WAS the One Who arranged it and begun it. Ephesians 3:9 says, "I was to make all men comprehend the significance of this mystery. God remained quiet about this mystery from the earliest starting point of the world. Furthermore, He is the One Who made all things." (Genesis 1:1;Deuteronomy 4:39; I Corinthians 8:6; II Corinthians 4:6).

God the Son brought it into being. Colossians 1:16 says, "Christ made everything that is seen and things that are not seen. He made every one of the forces of paradise.

Everything was made by Him and for Him." (John 1:1-3; I Corinthians 8:6; Hebrews 1:2;11:3).

God the Holy Spirit completed it. (Beginning 1:2; Job 26:13; 33:4).

It very well may be thought of along these lines: When a house is assembled, one designs how it is to be fabricated. Another forms the building, and another completions within. Each had a section. This can be found in Genesis 1:1-3, God the Father in verse 1, God the Spirit in verse 2, and God the Son in verse 3. God did not just make the world that is seen, He also made things that are not seen.

He made the blessed messenger that is found in Colossians 1:16, which says, "Christ made everything in the sky and on earth. He made everything that is seen and things that are not seen. He made every one of the forces of paradise. Everything was made by Him and for Him.

The Hebrew word for made is discovered multiple times in Genesis 1. In verse 1 - God made (produced using nothing) the sky and the earth. In verse 21 - He made creature life. In verse 26 - He made human life. Man has dependably wanted to realize God did these things, however He kept His ways a mystery.

A few people tragically think the things God made are God Himself. God ought not be venerated in what He has made. These things demonstrate that an All-amazing God made them, however men must not venerate them. Man must love the One Who made them. The inquiry is asked, for what reason did God (make things from nothing)? There is just a single answer. God made everything for His very own sparkling significance, similarly as He needed them, and for His very own utilization.

This is found in Revelation 4:11, "Our Lord and our God, it is appropriate for you to have the sparkling enormity and the respect and power. You made all things. They were made and have life since you liked it as such." (Nehemiah 9:6; Romans 11:36; Ephesians 1:5).

God Keeps And Takes Care Of Things He Made

COLOSSIANS 1:17 SAYS, "CHRIST was before all things." All things are held together by Him." Some individuals have tragically thought God has left the world to run itself. "The Son shines with the shining greatness of the Father. The Son Who holds up the entire world by the power of His Word.

The Son gave His very own life so we could be perfect from all wrongdoing (sin). After He had done that He sat down on the right side of God in paradise." This is the part Christ has in keeping things together and running great. Christ spoke about the feathered birds of the sky and the flowers of the field as being thought about by God. If He thinks about them, what amount more does He care for man? (Matthew 5:45; 6:26; 10:29-31).

God shows in His Word that He has made and is keeping things as He wants them.

1. The earth, sun, moon, and stars remain as they were arranged. (Psalm 119:89-91).

2. The countries of the world are the place God put them or where He enables them to be. Acts 17:26 says, "He produced using one blood all countries who live on the earth. He set the occasions and places where they should live." (Deuteronomy 32:8).

3. The length of human life is as God arranged it. Job 14:5 says, "A man's days are numbered. You know the quantity of his months: He can't live longer than the time You have set."

4. The demonstrations of man, both great and awful, are permitted by God. Luke 22:22 says, "The Son of Man will be taken along these lines since it has been in God's arrangement. In any case, it is terrible for that man who hands Him over!" (Acts 2:23; 4:27,28;Ephesians 2:10; I Peter 2:8; Revelation 17:17).

5. The saving of men from the punishment of wrongdoing (sin) is by God's arrangement. (Isaiah 53:5; Romans 8:29,30: Ephesians 1:3,10,11).

Chapter

EIGHT

The Holy Writings

The Holy Writings Came From God

THE BIBLE IS THE only written Word God has for people. This most noteworthy of all books, The Holy Bible does not simply have God's Word in it, it IS the Word of God. It is all of the Holy Writings of God in one Book. There are sixty-six unique books in the Bible. Thirty-nine of these are in the Old Testament and twenty-seven are in the New Testament.

God utilized around 40 unique (Holy Ghost) inspired men to compose what He instructed them to compose. The principal books were composed around 1,800 years previously Christ and the last ones were composed around 100 years after Christ's death. From the earliest starting point to the end it was 1,600 years. II Peter 1:20,21 says, "Comprehend this first: No piece of the Holy Writings was ever written up by man. No piece of the Holy compositions came long prior in light of what man needed to compose. Be that as it may, heavenly men who had a place with God spoke what the Holy Spirit let them know."

The Holy Writings were composed long ago. But then they were composed for all individuals and for all occasions. There has been no requirement for different compositions to be given from God after the initial ones since they were complete. God's Word has everything a man has to think about God, about Jesus Christ, about the Holy Spirit, about the path for a sinner to end up an offspring of God, about how to have tranquility (peace) in this life, and about eternal life. God has given us His Word in writing. It can never be annihilated. Matthew 24:35 says, "Paradise and earth will pass away, however My words won't pass away."

The Holy Writings In Two Parts: The Old Testament And The New Testament

THE WORD TESTAMENT IMPLIES that God promised to do certain things for His people. Afterward, this word came to mean the book which had these promises in it.

God has constantly needed people to worship Him. The Old Testament can be known as the Old Way of Worship. It is the same with the New Testament. It very well may be known as the New Way of Worship in light of the fact that the two different ways of worship are unique.

The first, or Old Way of Worship, was by an arrangement of laws or rules and the giving of creatures or different things on the sacred place (altar) as a demonstration of worship. In the New Way of Worship, Christ was given.

He was God's perfect gift. Christ was the special case Who could keep the old laws. At the point when man puts his trust in Christ, he gives God his true worship. (Jews 9:1-14).

The Old Testament

THE OLD TESTAMENT TELLS the beginning of the world and all that God made on it and around it. It tells how He gave His laws or tenets for living to His people. It tells how men lived in that day. Now and then they satisfied God and here and there they battled against Him. It advises how certain men could tell what might occur later on. Also, it tells how Christ, the Promised One, the Son of God, would come to save people from the punishment of their sins when they put their trust in Him.

The New Testament

THE NEW TESTAMENT TELLS of the birth, life, and death of Jesus Christ, and this occurred as it was let it knew would occur in the Old Testament by God's initial ministers. It tells the start of the church as it is known today. It recounts the issues of the new churches and what must be done to carry on an approach to please God. It tells what will occur before Christ comes to earth the second time and how it will occur.

The Bible Is:
"THE BOOK"

THE ENGLISH WORD "BIBLE" originates from the dialect in which the New Testament was composed. Bible means "BooK." About 500 years after the introduction of Christ, the Holy Books came to be classified "The Holy Bible."

In some cases the works in the Bible are known as the Scriptures which signifies "The Holy Writings." The first Christians called the Word of God "The Scriptures."

The Bible isn't just a book. It is "THE BOOK." It is the most imperative of all books in light of the One Who made it be composed, and what It has in it. The word "Holy" is before "Bible" and is utilized on the grounds that the "Word of God" is "truth" and It is set apart from every single other book as "God's Word" to people of all times.

Long ago God chose inspired men to record what He let them know. There were various men. They inhabited diverse occasions and at different places. Their lives were distinctive in light of the places where they lived. A considerable lot of them never saw one another. Their families were unique. God utilized men as men, not as machines. The works that were written down all concur with one another and demonstrate that they originated from the same "Person." That "Person was God."

How The Bible Came To Man

"The Bible Came To Man In A Powerful Way"

GOD HAS KEPT HIS Writings over the numerous years. The Old Testament was composed in the Hebrew dialect on animal skins. This was how it was kept until the point that books were printed. The New Testament books were composed in the Greek dialect on writing paper produced using papyrus perused that developed in Egypt.

For a long time the words of the Bible were composed single word at a time by hand. The primary Bible to be printed was 1454. The Kings James Bible was deciphered from the Greek and Hebrew dialects into the English dialect and imprinted in the year 1611. The Word of God has been put into various languages so people over all the world can understand it.

There Are False Writings That Sinful Men Try To Say Are The Word Of God

THERE ARE A FEW compositions that individuals have wanted to put in the Bible that are not God's Word. These false works must not be taken for God's Word.

Around 1,500 years prior the leaders of the church met to investigate these books and test them for truth. There are numerous false books that have been composed that resemble the Holy Writings. These false compositions have words in them that speak about God, yet they were not composed by holy men inspired by God (men God spoke through). The Holy Writings must not be added to or have words taken from them.

Deuteronomy 4:2 says, "Don't add to the Word that I let you know, and don't detract from it. Keep the laws of the Lord your God which I let you know." Revelation 22:18,19 says, "I am telling everybody who hears the words that are written in this book; If anybody adds anything to what is written in this book, God will add to him the kinds of trouble that this book tells about. In the event that anybody removes any piece of this book tells what will occur in the future, God will remove his part from the tree of life and from the Holy City which are written in this book."

How It Was Decided Which Writings Were God-Given And Made Alive By Him

THERE WERE CERTAIN MEN God chose to write His Word. However, there were other men who composed different compositions that looked much like God's Word, and some even endeavored to call these false works Holy works. Books that turned out to be a piece of the Bible needed to complete certain tests.

The books in the Old Testament must be composed, assembled, or discussed as true; by an early preacher. The Writings in the New Testament must be composed by one of the twelve men Jesus Christ tailed Him, or one who lived and worked with one of the followers of these men.

Help needed to originate from these Writings with the goal that people could develop in their Christian lives.

The Writings must be as of now being used by the places of worship and needed to have substantiated themselves.

The most critical test was if the book demonstrated that it was God-given and made alive by Him.

Everybody of the 66 books in the Bible today have experienced numerous tests. The 66 books that are in the Bible passed through the tests. Alternate works that did not pass through these equivalent tests are not put - and ought not be placed - in the Bible.

Why The Bible Was Written

THE MOST IMPORTANT REASON for the Bible being written was for God to tell people the things He wanted them to know. The Bible is God-Speaking.

God spoke in the Old Testament through exceptional evangelists who recorded what He let them know. Jews 1:1 says, "Long ago God addressed our initial fathers in numerous and distinctive ways, He spoke through the early preachers." (Luke 1:70; Acts 3:21; Romans 1:2). In the Old Testament He tells how the world and everything in it was made and how He helped his people, the Jews. The Old Testament additionally tells the news that He would send His Son, Jesus, at a later time. (Jeremiah 36:2,3; Ezekiel 1:3).

God spoke in the New Testament through Jesus. In Hebrews 1:2a it says, "Yet in these last days He (God) has spoken to us through His Son."

The New Testament tells about the birth of Jesus and His work while on earth. God's Word says numerous things in regards to individuals too. God needs man to realize he is a sinner. At that point God needs him to recognize what should be possible to be saved from the punishment of sin.

In Romans 6:20-23 it says, "When sin had power over your life, you were wrong with God. What great did you get from the things you are embarrassed about at this point? Those things bring death. However, now you are free from the power of sin. You have become a servant for God. Your life is set apart for God-like living. The end is life that keeps going forever. You get what is coming to you when you sin. It is passing (sying, death)! In any case, God's free gift is life that lasts forever. It is given to us by our Lord Jesus Christ.

When a man sees truth and puts his trust in Jesus Christ, he finds the Bible has much in it to enable him to carry on with his life in the right way. In II Timothy 3:16,17 it says, "All the Holy Writings are God-given and are made alive by Him.

Man is helped when he is shown God's Word. It demonstrates what isn't right. It changes the way for a man's life. It demonstrates to him proper ways to be right with God. It gives the man who has a place with God all that he needs to function admirably for Him."

At the point when a man wonders what the appropriate response is to issues he has throughout his life, he should peruse the Word of God. Incredible solace can be found in God's Word, and it advises everything man needs to know to live for God.

The Bible Was Written For Man To Learn About God

CHRISTIANS CAN LEARN SOMETHING by perusing the Bible over and over. The Holy Spirit enables man to comprehend what God is stating to him through the Bible. The Bible will enable Christians to develop to end up more grounded, stronger Christians. It is hard for a man to peruse a book when the room is getting dark. It is difficult to perceive what he is perusing. When he turns on the light, it turns out to be anything but difficult to peruse.

The equivalent is genuine when the Bible appears to be difficult to get it. When he asks the Holy Spirit to encourage him, it resembles a light to his mind making it less demanding for him to comprehend what he is reading.

The Bible isn't God, however it is God speaking. God has spoken and the Bible is His Word in writing to man. II Peter 1:20,21 says, "No piece of the Holy Writings was ever made up by any man. No piece of the Holy Writings came long ago due to what man needed to compose. Yet, holy men who had a place with God spoke (wrote) what the Holy Spirit let them know."

Chapter

NINE

The Holy Writings Are God-Given And Made Alive By Him

How the Holy Writings were given is hard to understand. No one knows all the answers.

God Gave His Word To Men To Write

At various occasions amid 1,600 Years 40 unique men were utilized of God to compose the sixty-six books of the Bible, yet it is just a single Book. It recounts the unparalleled way to be saved from sin, and the one way to paradise. No other religious book has such an arrangement. No other book has demonstrated all it contains is "true."

How the Holy Writings were given is difficult to understand. An exceptional power that isn't known today was given to the blessed men long ago who wrote down what God led them to write even to the plain words they should utilize. They were kept from committing an error and from forgetting anything that ought to have been composed. It was power given by the Holy Spirit but we don't know how it functioned.

This power was offered only to the men who composed the Holy Writings. This implies no other books are God's Holy Writings. The Holy Spirit led or guided them in what they composed and the words to utilize. This implies the first works had no missteps. (It is feasible for Bibles written in the dialect of today to have botches. Words in any dialect change in importance over numerous years, and in light of this a portion of the implications are not a similar today. It is critical that individuals make sure the Bible they read is consistent with the dialects the Bible was first written in.).

God Gave His Word To Man

GOD IS POWER, HOLY, pure, truth, and loaded with love, and has loving pity for the people He made. It very well may be seen wherever that He has made things for man to utilize. God offers air to relax, to breathe. God influences the seeds to develop and gives daylight and rain. God has given man the understanding about how to make these things give him what he needs.

Yet, man needs something other than these things. He has a sin issue! He feels regretful and realizes something isn't right in his heart. None of the things God made for man to use, or the understanding a man has can enable him to comprehend what to do about guilty feeling, or how to be right with God.

Man knows there is something more after this life. He should be prepared for eternal life.

God who gave man the various things he required, likewise made a path for him to know and see how he can be right with God. God gave man His Holy, Pure Word.

God's Word Is To Be Trusted

THE BIBLE, GOD'S WORD, is more important than any other religious book. It advises what man must be like to be right with God. It tells how terrible sin is and advises the sinner how to get right with God.

Two unique occasions God's Word recounts the simple words being composed by God and Christ. In Exodus 31:18 it says, "When the Lord had completed the process of speaking with Moses on Mount Sinai, He gave him the two stone works of the Law, bits of stone written on by the finger of God."

What's more, in John 8:6 it says, "Jesus got down and started to write in the dirt or dust with His finger." Both of these compositions were before long decimated. The bits of stone with the composed Law were broken before the children of Israel who were worshiping a false god, and it was not well before the people walked over what Jesus had written on the ground.

Yet, it pleased God to have His Law and the Good News of life that keeps going forever written through the Holy Spirit led men He chose for that special job.

Know that Jesus trusted and showed the Old Testament Writings. Not even once did He disclose to His followers they expected to keep an eye out for mix-ups in the Holy Writings. Jesus rushed to demonstrate the wrong-doings of the people of His day (Matthew 23). In Luke 9:35 it says, "Jesus turned and spoke sharp words to them. He stated, "You don't realize what sort of spirit you have.

The Son of Man did not come to destroy men's lives. He came to save them from the punishment of sin." It was simple for Him to get them straight in their reasoning about things so it would have been similarly as simple for Him to tell about specific mix-ups that got into the early Holy Writings which were not given by His Spirit, if there had been any.

Be that as it may, rather than this. He constantly utilized the Holy Writings, making it plain to the people that each word could be trusted. Matthew 5:18 says, "I let you know, as long as paradise and earth last, not one little mark or part of a word will pass away of the Law of Moses until the point that it has all been finished."

In Luke 21:22 it says, "All things will occur as it is written." Luke 24:44 it says, "Everything expounded on Me in the Law of Moses and in the Books of the early preachers and in the Psalm must occur as they said they would occur." Jesus utilized the words "The Law of Moses" and the "Books of the early preachers" and "the Psalms when discussing the Old Testament. Such words would not be utilized by Jesus if any parts were not given by the Holy Spirit or were not true.

The Bible Is God's Word – Not Man's Word

Thus, the Holy Writings were composed by men God chose for that activity. God's written Word was breathed upon and made alive by Him. As time went on, other men put these same words on different skins and on papyrus reed paper. The initial ones were decimated or lost. A portion of the ones made later are in a portion of the expansive urban communities of the world and can be read by the individuals who know the dialects in which they were written. Regardless we have with us today around 1,000 pieces of the Old Testament and around 4,000 pieces of the New Testament.

God's Word Is True

The Bible Is True Because God Says It Is True

The Bible is God's Word. God always tells the truth. So the Bible is genuine in light of the fact that it is God's Word. Psalm 119:89 says,

"Perpetually, O Lord, Your Word will never show signs of change in paradise." Psalm 119:160 says, "All of Your Word is truth, and all of Your laws, which are in every case right, will keep going forever." Isaiah 40:8 says, The grass dries up, The blossom loses its color. But the Word of our God stands forever."

The Bible Is True Because Jesus Believed It To Be True

JESUS KNEW THE HOLY Writings, now called the Old Testament. Jesus loved them, lived by them, preached them, constructed His lessons on them, considered them the "Fact of the matter," "God's Truth," and "God's Word." In Luke 4:4-12 when Jesus was tempted by the devil, He spoke words from the Holy Writings. In Luke 4:16-21 it says that Jesus read the Holy Writings at Nazareth. When petitioning God the Father, Jesus said in John 17:17b, "Your Word is truth." Jesus says in Matthew 24:35, "Paradise and earth will pass away, yet My words won't pass away."

Jesus said in John 10:35, "The Word of God can't be put aside." Jesus taught from the Holy

Writings since He trusted them. These are a portion of the things Jesus trusted that are told about in the Holy Writings:

God made man (Genesis 2:7; Matthew 19:4)

Marriage (Genesis 2:24; Matthew 19:5)

The Burning Bush (Exodus 3:4-6; Luke 20:37)

Moses (Exodus 20:1-21; Deuteronomy 25:5; Mark 7:10; 12:19-26)

The Blood of Abel (Genesis 4:8; Luke 11:51)

Noah and the flood (Genesis 6:5-7; Matthew 24:37-39)

Solomon and the Queen of Sheba (I Kings 10:1; Matthew 12:42)

Abraham, Isaac, Jacob (Exodus 3:6; Mark 12:26)

Lot, his wife, and the city of Sodom were destroyed (Genesis 19; Luke 17:28,29, 32)

The food God sent from paradise to the general population in the desert (Exodus 16:4,5; John 6:31,32, 49)

The snake on the .pole (Numbers 21:9; John 3:14)

Elijah and the long time everybody was without nourishment. The woman whose spouse had died at Zarepath. Naaman healed from an awful skin illness. (I Kings 17:1-9; II Kings 5:1-14; Luke 4:25-27)

Jonah in the fish (Jonah 1:17; Matthew 12:39-41; 16:4)

Jesus started His season of preaching on earth with the words, "It is written." (Matthew 4:4,7, 10) "Jesus stated, "You foolish men. How slow you are to believe what the early preachers have said" (Luke 24:25).

Jesus taught utilizing words from 22 books of the Old Testament. He instructed from the Holy Writings as Words from God. Not once did He detract from the words and from truth of them. He said that He didn't come to get rid of the Law of Moses or the Writings of the early preachers, "I have not come to do away with them but rather to finish them. I let you know, as long as paradise and earth last, not one little mark or part of a word will pass away of the Law of Moses until the point when it has all been done" (Matthew 5:17,18). Jesus realized that even the littlest letter utilized in composing God's Word was important.

The Bible Is True Because Many Of The Things It Said Would Happen Have Already Happened

THINGS HAPPENED IN THE life of Jesus that the Bible told about many years before Jesus was born.

Number of Years Before Jesus birth	Where it is found in the Old Testament	Where it happened in the New Testament in the life of Jesus	
1898 yrs.	Gen. 18:18	Born in Abraham's family	Acts 3:25
1898 yrs.	Gen. 17:19	Born in Isaac's family	Matt. 1:2
1452 yrs.	Num. 24:17	Born in Jacob's family	Luke 3:34
1689 yrs.	Gen. 49:10	Born in Judah's family	Luke 3:33
710 yrs.	Micah 5:2	Place of birth	Matt. 2:1

538 yrs.	Daniel 9:25	Time of birth	Luke 2:1,2
742 yrs. .	Isaiah 7:14	Born of a woman who never had a man	Matt. 1:18
487yrs.	Zech. 11:12	Sold for 30 pieces of silver-	Matt.26:15
712 yrs.	Isaiah 53:12	On the cross beside sinners	Matt.27:38
1050 yrs.	Psalm 109:4	Prays for enemies	Luke 23:34
1050 yrs.	Psalm 34:20	Not a bone broken	John 19:33,36
1050 yrs.	Psalm 16:10	Raised From the dead	Matt. 28:9

God's Word also tells numerous things about the Jewish nation. Things that were told many years ago have come true.

The Bible Is True Because The Way It Was Written Shows It Is The Word Of God

A LARGE PORTION OF the men who composed the books of the Bible had never seen one another. A portion of the men even talked distinctive dialects and lived in various nations. A portion of the men were shepherds. Some were kings. One made tents. One was a doctor and one was a tax authority (collector). However all aspects of the Bible concurs with every single other part. Just the All-amazing God could have led every one of these men to think of one Book.

The Bible Is True Because Of The Way It Changes Lives

NO OTHER BOOK HAS done the things the Bible has done. The Bible recounts the main path for man to have peace with God. It tells how man must be conceived once more (born again). God's great power can be seen changing lives when individuals read and obey what the Bible teaches. The Bible advises how man can come to God.

Jesus says that He is the Way and the Truth and the Life. He says that nobody can go to the Father except by Him. (John 14:6).

The Bible Is True Because It Has Never Been Or Never Can Be Destroyed

A FEW MEN HAVE attempted to destroy the Bible. A few men attempted to consume every one of the duplicates of the Bible. Individuals have been executed with much torment for having a Bible. However, the more men attempt to decimate the Bible, the more it is read, believed and accepted.

The Bible Is True Because Truth Never Changes

BOOKS HAVE BEEN COMPOSED by men lose their significance as the years pass by. The Bible still has significance and truth to all who perused it today. Just as much as it did for those who first read it years ago.

Bibliography

The Holy Bible (1964) Authorized King James Version. Chicago, Ill.: J. G. Ferguson

The Holy Bible (1953) The Revised Standard Version. Nashville, TN.: Thomas Nelson And Sons (Used By Permission)

The Holy Bible (1901) The American Standard Version. Nashville, Tn.: Thomas Nelson (Used By Permission)

The Holy Bible (1959) The Berkeley Version. Grand Rapids, MI.: Zondervan (Used By Permission)

The Holy Bible (2017) The New Testament Version. Grand Rapids, MI.: Zondervan (Used By Permission)

The New Testament In Modern English (1958) J. B. Philips, New York, NY: Macmillian (Used By Permission)

The New Testament In The Language Of The People (1937, 1949) Chicago, Ill.: Charles B. Williams, Bruce Humphries, Inc. Moody Bible Institute (Used By Permission)

About The Author

The Reverend Dr. John Thomas Wylie is one who has dedicated his life to the work of God's Service, the service of others; and being a powerful witness for the Gospel of Our Lord and Savior Jesus Christ. Dr. Wylie was called into the Gospel Ministry June 1979, whereby in that same year he entered The American Baptist College of the American Baptist Theological Seminary, Nashville, Tennessee.

As a young Seminarian, he read every book available to him that would help him better his understanding of God as well as God's plan of Salvation and the Christian Faith. He made a commitment as a promising student that he would inspire others as God inspires him. He understood early in his ministry that we live in times where people question not only who God is; but whether miracles are real, whether or not man can make a change, and who the enemy is or if the enemy truly exists.

Dr. Wylie carried out his commitment to God, which has been one of excellence which led to his earning his Bachelors of Arts in Bible/Theology/Pastoral Studies. Faithful and obedient to the call of God, he continued to matriculate in his studies earning his Masters of Ministry from Emmanuel Bible College, Nashville, Tennessee & Emmanuel Bible College, Rossville, Georgia. Still, inspired to please the Lord and do that which is well – pleasing in the Lord's sight, Dr. Wylie recently on March 2006, completed his Masters of Education degree with a concentration in Instructional Technology earned at The American Intercontinental University, Holloman Estates, Illinois. Dr. Wylie also previous to this, earned his Education Specialist Degree from Jones International University, Centennial, Colorado and his Doctorate of Theology from The Holy Trinity College and Seminary, St. Petersburg, Florida.

Finally, Reverend Dr. Wylie is devoted to publishing books that spread the gospel of Jesus Christ, helping Christians to live as per that gospel, advance restoration, revival in the church, give testimony regarding Jesus Christ, Christian Unity and Fellowship in Christian Love.

Dr. Wylie has served in the capacity of pastor at two congregations in Middle Tennessee and Southern Tennessee, as well as served as an

Evangelistic Preacher, Teacher, Chaplain, Christian Educator, and finally a published author, writer of many great inspirational Christian Publications such as his first publication: *"Only One God: Who Is He?" – published August 2002 via formally 1st books library (which is now AuthorHouse Book Publishers located in Bloomington, Indiana & Milton Keynes, United Kingdom)* which caught the attention of **The Atlanta Journal Constitution Newspaper.**

Dr. Wylie is happily married to Angel G. Wylie, a retired Dekalb Elementary School teacher who loves to work with the very young children and who always encourages her husband to move forward in the Name of Jesus Christ. They have Four children, 11 grand-children and one great-grandson of whom they are very proud. Both Dr. Wylie and Angela Wylie serve as members of the Salem Baptist Church, located in Lilburn, Georgia, where the Reverend Dr. Richard B. Haynes is Senior pastor.

Dr. Wylie has stated of his wife: "she knows the charm and beauty of sincerity, goodness, and purity through Jesus Christ. Yes, she is a Christian and realizes the true meaning of loveliness as the reflection as her life of holy living gives new meaning, hope, and purpose to that of her husband, her children, others may say of her, "Behold the handmaiden of the Lord." A Servant of Jesus Christ!

About The Book

THIS PUBLICATION, "THERE IS One True And Living God," does not endeavor to demonstrate there is a God but rather has inside it's pages the things that assist men to know "there is one true and living God."

The Bible being God's disclosure or God's revelation to man, God speaks from the very first page. The Bible does not address the presence of God by unique thinking, however starts with the simple act of Creation.

Again, the Bible does not endeavor to show that there is a God. Men wherever definitely know there is a God. One Who is head over "all things". But then, individuals ponder about Who this God is and might want to know many things about Him.

The Bible is the authority! The Bible is God's spoken Word, written by inspired men of God.

Reverend Dr. John Thomas Wylie

Printed in the United States
By Bookmasters